CHAOS

A Collection of Poems
Lessons on Life, and Love

MEME LUKWITZ-MIHALOVIC

ARCHWAY
PUBLISHING

Archway Publishing books may be ordered through booksellers or by contacting:

Archway Publishing
1663 Liberty Drive
Bloomington, IN 47403
www.archwaypublishing.com
844-669-3957

ISBN: 978-1-6657-6118-5 (sc)
ISBN: 978-1-6657-6120-8 (hc)
ISBN: 978-1-6657-6119-2 (e)

Library of Congress Control Number: 2024911555

Print information available on the last page.

Archway Publishing rev. date: 06/25/2024

DEDICATION

To my parents for all their love, encouragement, and support in everything I do.

To my kids, J, A, S, and C and my grandson thank you for making me a mom/grandma. For loving and giving me strength. This momma bear loves you to the moon and back.

To D.W. thank you for inspiring me pick up my pen again.

Love you all
M

CONTENTS

WHY YOU SHOULD HIRE ME

Why should you hire me? Let me count the ways.
For I am an advocate in every sense of the word,
A voice for those who remain unheard,
With passion and conviction, I'll fight for what's right,
Ensuring justice prevails, both day anid night.

I am a servant leader, humble in my approach,
Putting others before myself, a servant to encroach,
With empathy and kindness, I'll guide with care,
In building a team that's strong and fair.

A problem solver, I'll tackle any task,
With a mind that's sharp, ready to unmask
The challenges that lay ahead, I'll face them head-on,
Finding solutions until they're gone.

But I'm not just a solver, I'm a cheerleader too,
Supporting and uplifting in all that I do,
With a smile on my face, and words of encouragement,
I'll inspire those around me, to reach their full extent.

Approachable, you'll find me open and warm,
A listening ear in the midst of any storm,
Ready to offer guidance, advice, and support,
Creating an atmosphere where ideas can be explored.

Curiosity drives me, a thirst for knowledge untamed,
I'll explore new territories, unafraid and unashamed,
Seeking to learn, grow, and expand my horizons
Uncovering new perspectives in life's endless seasons.

A community builder, I'll foster connections that thrive,
Bringing people together, like bees to a hive,
Creating a space where cooperation can bloom,
Where ideas can flourish, and innovation can balloon.

Authenticity is my mantra, I wear it on my sleeve,
Being true to myself in all that I believe,
With honesty and integrity, I'll always stay true,
A genuine soul, you can trust me through and through.

I'll think outside the box, break free from the norm,
Creativity unleashed, a powerful storm,
Exploring unconventional paths with an open mind,
Unearthing possibilities we never thought we'd find.

But above all, I'll encourage one and all
To reach for the stars, to rise, to stand tall,
A motivator, an inspiration, I'll be your guiding light,
Together, we'll conquer any challenge in sight.

So, why should you hire me? The answer is clear:
I bring a unique blend of qualities,
An advocate, a servant leader, a problem solver too,
A cheerleader, approachable, curious, and true.

With an open mind and heart, I'll lead the way
In building a team that's strong, come what may,
So, take a chance on me, and together we shall see
The heights we can reach, when you hire me.

PEBBLES BENEATH MY FEET

The pebbles beneath my feet,
As I walked along the shore.
Cold water lapping over my toes,
Whispering secrets from afar.

With each step, a gentle rhythm,
A dance between earth and sea.
In harmony they intertwine,
Creating a symphony for just me.

The salty breeze kisses my cheeks,
As I stroll along the sandy way.
The sun whispered through the clouds,
Welcoming the promise of a brand-new day.

In the distance, children's laughter,
Like music in the summer air.
Their joy contagious, infectious,
Filling my heart with a love so rare.

I walked along, immersed in bliss,
Not a soul beside me there.
While enveloped by nature's grace,
I found solace beyond compare.

The pebbles whispered ancient tales
Of journeys taken, dreams untold.
They carried the weight of countless years,
Yet offered comfort, like a hand to hold.

And as I wandered, lost in thought,
I realized the truth so clear.
That in the presence of nature's wonders,
Loneliness simply disappears.

For nature is a faithful friend,
A companion that never leaves.
In its embrace, I find solace,
A refuge where my soul believes.

So, I walked along not alone,
But with the earth beneath my feet.
Connected to all that surrounded me,
In this moment, life feels complete.

MEME LUKWITZ-MIHALOVIC

KIND EYES

You have kind eyes,
They crinkle and twinkle when you laugh,
You have joy in your life
Because you bring joy to so many,
Laughter and joy, but is there peace?

In the depths of those gentle orbs,
I see a world seeking solace,
A yearning for tranquility,
Amidst life's chaotic race.

Your eyes hold stories untold
Of battles fought within,
A spirit that longs for respite,
From the noise under your skin.

For in your laughter's melodic ring,
I sense echoes of a weary soul,
A heart burdened with the weight
Of a world that takes its toll.

Yet you persist, a beacon of light,
Defying the shadows that loom,
With every smile you bestow,
You sow seeds of hope to bloom.

Your kindness, a balm for wounded hearts,
A salve that eases pain,
You weave compassion into your words,
Leaving trails of love in your wake.

But peace, elusive as a fleeting dream,
Does it elude your grasp too?
As you navigate life's winding streams,
Do you yearn for serenity anew?

In the depths of your kind eyes,
I glimpse a silent plea
For harmony to dance in your soul
And set your spirit free.

May you find solace in stillness,
Amidst life's relentless race,
May peace embrace your weary heart,
And kindness guide your every trace.

For your laughter and joy are precious,
Yet peace is just as dear,
May your kind eyes find tranquility,
And let serenity draw near.

IMAGINATION, DOODLES, AND LINES

In the realm of imagination's canvas,
Doodles dance upon the canvas,
Miscellaneous drawings, a tapestry of dreams,
Whispers of thought untamed and free.

Lines meander, like rivers bending,
Creating shapes, they intertwine,
A collection of sketches, an artist's treasure,
Each stroke a story waiting to be unveiled.

In the realm of colors, hues converge,
Brushes dipped in vibrant shades,
Can doodles, drawings and sketches,
Become images with some special meaning?

They speak in whispers, these humble lines,
Revealing secrets unseen by naked eyes,
A symphony of strokes, a silent conversation,
Unveiling worlds beyond our comprehension.

From mere scribbles, they take their flight,
Transforming paper into portals of delight,
Abstract forms, they find their voice:
A language untamed with no defined choice.

Faces emerge, emotions unfold,
As graphite dances, stories are told,
In the quiet corners of a sketchbook's page,
A world imagined takes center stage.

A doodle's journey, like a wandering muse,
Unpredictable, yet always infused,
With the essence of the artist's soul,
Each stroke a fragment, creating the whole.

So let us cherish those spontaneous creations,
For in their chaos lies profound elation,
Doodles, drawings, and sketches intertwined,
Bearing witness to the boundless human mind.

For in the realm of imagination's stroke,
Doodles become masterpieces, evoking hope,
A collection of sketches, a glimpse of our being,
Images with meaning forever freeing.

A FLAME THAT FLICKERS

In the realm of desire, an ember burns,
A flame that flickers, yearning to be known,
Looks of longing, a language all its own,
Igniting hearts with passions that return.

Oh, burning desire, the sweetest affliction,
Unleashing floods of fervor uncontained,
Deep, unending kisses, souls unchained,
Merging, two bodies in perfect fusion.

No rhythm confines this passionate dance,
For in free verse, desire finds its voice,
No rules or boundaries to stifle its choice,
A symphony of yearning, a wild romance.

In this realm, bodies melded together,
Freed from the shackles of societal norms,
Unveiling the depths where passion transforms,
A love so fierce, it defies all tether.

Through every touch, a story unfolds,
A tale of yearning, fierce and unbound,
Surrendering to desires that astound,
In the embrace where passion beholds.

So let desire burn, unquenchable flame,
Let the looks of longing guide the way
In this realm, where hearts forever stray,
Finding solace in each other's name.

RUNAWAY TRAIN

My mind is like a runaway train,
Wheels spinning round and round,
Thoughts going to and fro,
Just like a runaway train.

No conductor to guide its path,
No brakes to slow its speed,
It roams the vast expanse of my consciousness,
Without direction or heed.

Through valleys of memories it races,
Past fields of dreams and hopes,
It chases elusive desires
And collides with fears and doubt.

Sometimes it speeds on the tracks of joy,
Leaping over hurdles of sadness,
But then it derails into the ravines of despair,
Lost in a wilderness of madness.

It carries me to distant lands.
Where imagination knows no bounds,
I witness the beauty of creation,
And explore the depths of the profound.

But in its chaotic journey,
It can cause destruction and pain,
Hurting those who dare to board,
This runaway train in my brain.

MEME LUKWITZ-MIHALOVIC

Yet amidst the chaos and noise,
I find solace in the poetic refrain,
For within this runaway train of mine,
Lies the essence of my creative domain.

So I'll embrace the wild ride,
With its twists and turns untamed.
For in the depths of this runaway train,
Lies the freedom that cannot be named.

My mind is like a runaway train,
Wheels spinning around and around,
Thoughts going to and fro,
Just like a runaway train.

DEPTHS OF SORROW

In the depths of sorrow's embrace,
A journey through the shadows we trace,
Loss of a mother, a guiding light,
Now lost in the depths of eternal night.

Gone is the laughter, the tender touch,
Memories linger, they hurt so much,
A void in the heart, aching and raw,
The weight of absence, a heavy straw.

Loss of a grandmother, wise and kind,
Her words like whispers, forever imprinted in mind,
Her love, a shelter in life's stormy sea,
Now a treasure lost, forever to be.

A daughter's absence, a painful sting,
A bond once strong, now a broken thing,
The grief runs deeps, a river unbound,
In the depths of sorrow, we are drowned.

Clouds hang heavy, casting shadows wide,
The sun obscured, no solace to provide,
But know, dear heart, that through the darkest haze,
The sun will shine again to brighter days.

With time, the clouds will scatter and fade,
And healing whispers will serenade,
For in every loss, a seed is sown,
To bloom anew, a strength unknown.

MEME LUKWITZ-MIHALOVIC

Though the pain may linger and the ache endures,
The heart will mend, love will endure,
Embrace the memories, hold them tight,
For in the darkness, they'll be your light.

Loss of mother, grandmother, daughter,
The sadness of loss, the tears that water,
Yet as time moves on, the sun will shine,
And love's embrace will again be thine.

BEAUTY'S ENCOUNTER

Did you see that beautiful sunrise
With the hues of gold and amber that rise?
A glimpse of beauty's gentle surprise
Unveiling secrets under painted skies.

Did you see that magnificent sunset,
Where the horizon and colors meet?
A glimpse of beauty's gentle surprise
Unveiling secrets under painted skies.

Embrace the mystery that unfolds,
Beauty in nature, stories untold
With each dawn and dusk, behold
The wonders of beauty, pure and bold.

In the realm where beauty reigns supreme,
Transcending time like in a surreal dream,
Let it whisper softly in the gleam
Of sunsets and sunrises, a captivating stream.

FUCK MY HEART

Fuck, Fuck, Fuck!
The words keep flying out
But they can't capture
The depths of this doubt

You have a hold on my heart
A grip that won't let go
I try to break free
But the pull is too strong, I know

You were once my everything
My reason to live
But now you're my nightmare
The pain that I can't forgive

I hate the hold you have
The power you wield
You're like a poison
That I just can't shield

I wish I could forget you
Erase you from my mind
But every time I try
Your memory I find

Fuck, Fuck, Fuck!
Why did I ever let you in?
Now your presence lingers
A constant, painful sin

I hate that I still love you
Despite the hurt and pain
But I'll keep fighting
Until my heart can break your chain

So Fuck, Fuck, Fuck.
I'll say it one last time
But this time it's for me
To finally leave you behind.

IN THE SHADOW OF GRIEF

In the shadow of grief's heavy cloak,
Lies the rate of countless hearts that broke.
For in this realm of sorrow and pain,
A multitude of losses, like droplets of rain.

First, the loss of a cherished wife,
A partner, a lover, the center of your life,
Her absence, a void that can never be filled,
A love so profound, forever distilled.

Next, the loss of a nurturing mother,
Whose tender touch could calm any bother,
Her guiding light now dimmed and gone,
Leaving behind a sorrowful throng.

Then, the loss of a grandmother dear,
Whose warmth and wisdom will always be near,
Memories of laughter, stories shared,
Now treasures to cherish, for she is no longer there.

The loss of a daughter, so young and bright,
Snatched away in the depths of night,
A future so promising now forever lost,
Leaving hearts shattered, forever embossed.

And the loss of a sister, a bond so strong,
A friendship that should have carried on,
A companion, a confidante, forever missed
Her absence a void that cannot be kissed.

The sadness of loss, an eternal refrain,
A symphony of tears, an unending pain,
Clouds hang heavy obscuring the light,
But through the darkness hope shines bright.

For the sun will rise, chasing away the gray,
With each passing day, a step toward a brighter way,
Though the ache may linger deep in your core,
Life finds a way to bloom once more.

In the dappled light of memories made,
Strength is found in love's serenade,
And as the sunbeams dance upon our face,
We find solace in the warmth and embrace.

So, let us mourn, let us grieve,
For in our losses, we must believe
That through the tears and the cloudy haze,
Hope will guide us to brighter days.

MEME LUKWITZ-MIHALOVIC

SECOND CHANCES

Second chances—
A path to redemption
In the realm of loves lost,
And hearts torn asunder.

Second loves—
A gentle breeze,
Whispering hope,
In the hollows of our souls.

Second marriages—
A dance of two souls,
Waltzing through time,
With scars as reminders.

Second chances of losing love—
A bitter taste,
Of what could have been,
But wasn't meant to be.

In the tapestry of life,
Second chances weave
Threads of resilience
And the courage to believe.

For in the depths of darkness,
Love's light may yet shine,
Guiding us towards forgiveness,
And a love that's more divine.

So let us embrace
The beauty of the second,
For in the tapestry of life,
There lies a chance to mend.

MEME LUKWITZ-MIHALOVIC

MORNING HAS BROKEN

Morning has broken,
The sky is bright with hues of
Purple, orange, and pink
White clouds painting the sky

Day has broken with a beautiful blue sky
Big billowing clouds with the sun
Providing us with its warmth

Evening has downed upon us
With the setting sun casting
Reds, yellows, and ambers

Night has fallen
With its inky black sky
Dripping with stars

In this vast expanse of time and space
Nature unveils her ever-changing face

Morning awakens with a gentle touch
Sunlight spills, colors bloom, oh so much
A canvas painted in glorious array
As the world stirs, embracing the day

Clouds dance across the endless blue
Whispering secrets, revealing truths
Silent messengers of the sky above
Carrying dreams on wings of love

Evening arrives with a fiery grace
The sun descends, casting its embrace
A symphony of colors, a dazzling sight
A tapestry woven with celestial might

Night envelops a cloak of ebony
The stars emerge, jewels in the galaxy
Bathing the world in their sliver glow
Guiding lost souls where dreams may flow

From dawn to dusk, the cycle unfolds
Nature's story in the sky is told
Morning, noon, evening, and night
Each moment a gift, a wondrous delight

So let us cherish these moments divine
As the world spins, as the sun doth shine
For in each passing day a miracle's seen
In the sky's ever-changing captive scene.

MEME LUKWITZ-MIHALOVIC

MUSIC

Music is a constant–
Ever-present, never fading,
It weaves into the very fabric of our existence.
With each note it takes over our soul,
Captivating our senses, igniting our emotions.

Music can be soft–
A gentle whisper that caresses our ears,
Carrying us to realms of tranquility and peace.
Or it can be bold–
A thunderous roar that shakes the ground beneath our feet,
Awakening our spirits, stirring our passions.

Music can be techno–
A symphony of electronic pulses and beats,
Creating a rhythm that pumps through our veins.
Or it can be loving–
A tender melody that serenades our hearts,
Expressing emotions that words fail to convey.

Music is melodic–
A harmonious blend of sounds and tones,
Painting a masterpiece of audial beauty.
But above all music is the soul of being–
An intricate tapestry of stories and emotions,
Reflecting the joys, sorrows, and triumphs of our lives.

In each verse and chorus,
It speaks the language of our hearts,
Connecting us in ways nothing else can.
Through every rhythm and melody,
It tells the tale of our existence,
Weaving together the threads of our shared humanity.

So, let us embrace the gift,
Let us dance to its rhythm,
Sing its lyrics and feel its vibrations.
For in music, we find solace.
A sanctuary where our souls can truly soar,
And where the story of our lives finds its voice.

KINDNESS AND MAGIC

Kindness and magic intertwined in poetic grace,
Art seeks to provoke emotions we can't erase.
Artists, the feelers of the world, with hearts so bold,
Dreamers who dare to dream big stories yet untold.

In strokes of vibrant colors, their visions come alive,
A canvas filled with passion, where dreams and talents thrive,
With every stroke and every line, they weave a tale so true,
A tapestry of emotions creating magic anew.

Kindness, the brush that paints compassion's gentle hue,
A touch that heals the broken, a love that shines so true.
In acts of selflessness, they sprinkle stardust 'round,
Transforming lives with tender care in silence without a sound.

Artist and kindness, two forces intertwined,
Guided by the unseen, their spirits unconfined.
With every masterpiece they create, they touch our very souls,
A symphony of beauty and love, making us feel whole.

So let us celebrate these dreamers, these artists of the heart,
Whose kindness and magic, create a world of art.
For in their hands, they hold the power to inspire,
To ignite the spark within us all, and to set our souls on fire.

LIFE AND LOVE

Life and love,
Both are risky,
Like a delicate walk on a tightrope,
Balanced between joy and pain.

Life, unpredictable and wild,
Throws its challenges with abandon,
Testing our strength and resilience,
Pushing us to the edge of our limits.

Love, a beautiful enigma,
Whispering promises in the wind,
Filling our hearts with hope,
Yet shattering them with a single blow.

We take leaps of faith,
Knowing the risks that lie ahead,
For without risk there is no reward,
No chance for growth or true connection.

Life and love,
A dance of uncertainty,
Where we stumble and fall,
But also find moments of pure bliss.

In the face of danger, we embrace,
Knowing that the greatest joys
Often come from a place of vulnerability,
From opening our hears to the unknown.

So let us embrace the risk,
Hold hands with life and love,
For it is in the daring uncertain
That we truly find our purpose and worth.

MIRROR GAZE

In the mirror's gaze, what do you see?
Perfection's illusion or truth set free?
For we are human, bound in imperfections,
In this reflection, our deepest introspections.

Do you see flawless beauty untouched by time?
Or flaws that whisper, weaving tales sublime?
In every line and scar, a story resides,
A testament to strength, where resilience abides.

Oh mirror, mirror, reveal the truth within,
Beyond the surface, where judgments begin.
Through each imperfection, can we truly find,
The essence of our souls, unburdened and aligned?

Within each blemish, a journey unfolds,
Lessons learned, and stories untold.
For through the cracks, our light does shine,
Embracing imperfection, our spirits intertwine.

In this reflection, let judgment dissolve,
And self-acceptance, may it evolve.
For what we see in the mirror's embrace
Is a beautiful soul, seeking its own grace.

So, search not for perfection, but for love's embrace,
Embrace the imperfections, let them leave no trace.
For in the mirror's gaze, a truth we can't deny,
We are imperfect beings, yet beautifully alive.

MEME LUKWITZ-MIHALOVIC

YOUR SMILE HAD ME FROM THE START

Your smile had me from the start,
Its radiance, a work of art,
Your eyes laugh and it melts my heart,
A glimpse of joy, a perfect part.

Then you said, "Hello," and I was gone,
Lost in the music of your voice, a sweet song,
A symphony of emotions, a love reborn,
Hello again, my love, in this moment we belong.

Time stands still as we embrace,
Our souls entwine a divine chase,
Every word you speak a gentle grace,
In your presence, I find my solace, my sacred space.

Your laughter echoes a melody so pure,
It echoes through my being forever to endure,
With every note my love for you soars,
In your happiness my heart finds cure.

Hello again, my love, a greeting so dear,
Through life's journey I'm glad you're near,
With every hello, our connection grows sincere,
Together we'll face the world conquering every fear.

Your smile had me from the start,
Your eyes a reflection of love's art,
With each hello, we'll never be apart,
Hello again, my love, forever in my heart.

STOP THE HORRIBLE STORY

How do you stop telling
Your horrible story?
If you stop speaking the words,
Will the hurt cease to exist?
Will the pain evaporate,
Like mist in the morning sun?

Or will the signs persist,
Haunting your every step,
Like shadows in the night?
Will they continue to whisper,
Echoing through your mind,
Even when your voice is silenced?

Sometimes, the weight of the tale
Presses heavily upon your chest,
Threatening to suffocate,
To consume every breath of hope,
But perhaps, just maybe,
By releasing the grip on those words,
You can lighten the burden,
Allowing a sliver of healing to seep in.

For it is in the retelling
That the wound can fester,
Feeding on the rawness,
Gaining strength in the darkness,
Yet in the absence of their potency,
Their grip on your soul
And gradually fade into the abyss.

MEME LUKWITZ-MIHALOVIC

But, dear friend, take heed,
For the signs may persist,
Even when the story is no longer spoken,
They may appear as whispers in the wind
Or a gentle nudge from within,
Reminders of the battles fought,
And the strength gained.

So how do you stop telling
Your horrible story?
Perhaps you don't,
Instead, you transform it,
Mold it into something new:
A testament of resilience,
A bridge to empathy and understanding.
For within the depth of your pain
Lies a story of survival,
Of scars that have healed,
And wounds that have closed,
A testament to your strength
And the power of your spirit.

So tell your story my friend,
But rewrite it with love and compassion,
Infuse it with hope and redemption,
And watch as it transforms
From a tale of darkness
Into a beacon of light.

STARS

Stars to guide you,
Stars to remind you,
Like holes in the sky,
They twinkle and shimmer,
Guiding your journey
Through the dark unknown.

Their light a beacon,
Leading you forward
Through life's winding paths,
They hold secrets untold,
Whispering tales of hope,
In the depths of the night.

Stars, like distant friends,
Glowing from afar,
They watch over you
With gentle guiding hands,
Their celestial dance,
A tapestry of dreams.

Yet still, they offer solace,
A reminder of love's endurance,
For within their luminous embrace,
We find strength to carry on,
To navigate life's vast expanse
With courage and resilience.

MEME LUKWITZ-MIHALOVIC

So let the stars be your compass
In this vast cosmic sea,
Let them be your guiding light
When darkness clouds your way,
For they are there to remind you
That you're never truly alone.

THREE HOURS

Three hours of sleep,
Now I am wide awake,
The insomnia, boy, how it sucks,
And fucks up your life.

In the stillness of night,
I lie here restless, eyes staring
At the shadows dancing on the walls
As time slowly passes by.

Silent whispers echo within,
Thoughts swirl, tangled and entwined,
A cacophony of worries and fears
Keep sleep at bay, denying respite.

The world slumbers in tranquil bliss
While I battle the demons within,
Counting the seconds until dawn,
Yearning for the solace of dreams.

Oh, how cruel is this affliction,
Stealing away precious hours,
Leaving me in a haze of exhaustion,
Lost in the depths of fatigue.

My mind aches for sweet surrender,
To drift away on gentle waves,
But sleep eludes, slipping through my grasp,
Leaving me trapped in this waking nightmare.

Yet, amidst the darkness that engulfs,
A flicker of hope ignites,
For even in the depths of the despair,
Strength emerges resilient and bright.

I embrace the night as my companion,
Eyes wide open to the world's wonders,
In these hours of solitude,
I find solace in the beauty of the stars.

Through the weariness I prevail,
Finding strength in the depths of my being,
For even with three hours of sleep,
I rise determined, ready to face the day.

YESTERDAY WHEN IT WAS ONLY TOMORROW

Yesterday when it was only tomorrow
Was a sad and gloomy day
With shadows that lingered heavy and low
In a world that had lost its way.

The sun refused to shine its golden rays
And clouds draped the sky in gray
No laughter echoed no songs were sung
As darkness held its sway.

The flowers wilted, their colors faded
Their beauty hidden from view
The birds ceased their melodies
In a silence that pierced me through.

The whispers of hope were drowned by despair
As dreams were cast aside
For uncertainty ruled with an iron fist
And joy was denied.

But amidst the sorrow and the tears
There flickered a tiny flame
A glimmer of light, a spark of resilience
That refused to yield to the shame

For deep within our weary hearts
A strength began to grow
A determination to rise above
And let our spirits show.

MEME LUKWITZ-MIHALOVIC

Yesterday when it was only tomorrow
May have been filled with pain
But it ignited a fire within our souls
That can never be contained.

So let us embrace the challenges ahead
With courage in our stride
For yesterday's darkness has made us strong
And tomorrow we shall not hide.

END OF OUR RAINBOW

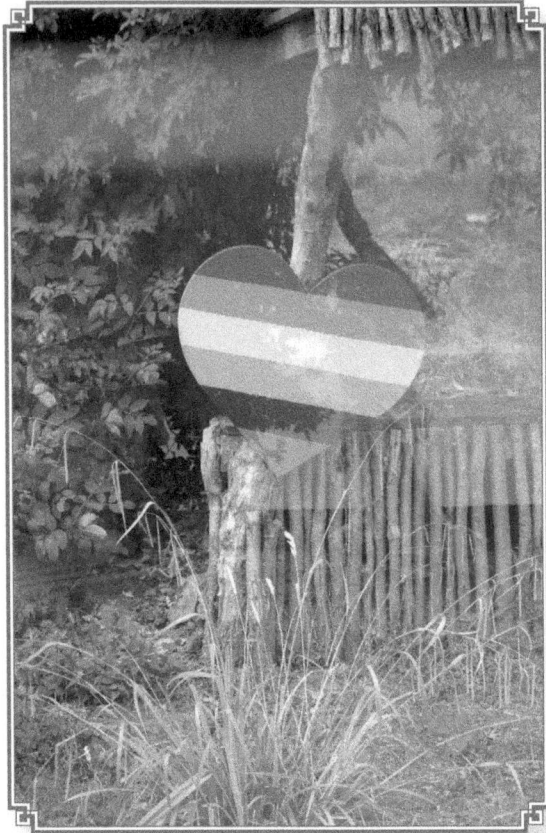

Yesterday we came to the end of our rainbow,
The colors all faded together from our tears.
In the wake of love's demise, we stand
Bereft of hope dashed our hearts torn.

Once we danced amidst a vibrant spectrum:
Each hue a promise of forever's embrace
But time, that cruel thief, stifles our laughter,
Leaving us stranded in a desolate place.

MEME LUKWITZ-MIHALOVIC

The red of passion turned to fiery rage
As our love burned in the heart of our fights,
Orange, once warm and comforting,
Now a flame that consumed our nights.

Yellow, the color of sunshine and joy,
Became pale, a mere flicker of its former glow.
Green envy crept into our hearts
As doubts and suspicions began to grow.

Blue, the shade of tranquility and calm,
Drowned beneath waves of sorrow and regret.
Indigo dreams turned to nightmares
As we struggled to forgive but couldn't forget.

And finally violet, the color of love's essence,
Faded, lost in the depths of our despair,
Our once vibrant rainbow, now a somber tapestry.
A reminder of the love we failed to repair.

Yesterday we came to the end of our rainbow
The colors all faded together from our tears
But let us not dwell on the past's bitter sting
For tomorrow holds the promise of new frontiers.

Let us learn from the mistakes that we made
And paint a new rainbow with hope's gentle stroke
May forgiveness and understanding guide our way
As we mend our hears and heal what was broke.

And perhaps in time a new rainbow will emerge
With colors brighter and more beautiful than before
For love's journey is never truly finished
It simply transforms, evolves, and opens new doors

Yesterday we came to the end of our rainbow
But today let us embrace the chance to start anew
With strength and resilience, we'll find our way
And create a love that's vibrant, honest, and true.

AS WE WALKED ALONG

As I walked along the snow covered path
Alongside the train tracks and the tranquil lake
A melancholy whisper wove through the air
And I couldn't help but feel my heart ache.

With each step memories danced before my eyes
Of sunrise's golden hues and sunset's fiery glow
Moments we shared, dreams we once held dear
Now lost as the frigid winds began to blow.

The snowflakes, like fragile dreams, gently fell
Blanketing the earth in a shimmering white
But the warmth we once shared now distant and cold
I yearned for your presence craving its light.

But fate had played its cruel hand upon us
And now I trudge this path alone my dear
The echoes of our laughter carried by the wind
Lost in the vastness fading forever unclear.

The train tracks stretched ahead leading nowhere
A parallel to the journey of my broken heart
Time had carved deep grooves leaving scars
As the train of life rumbles tearing us apart.

Yet, amidst the solitude that surrounded me
A newfound strength began to take its hold
For in the stillness I found solace and peace
An inner resilience, strong and bold

The snow-covered path became my companion
Whispering tales of resilience and grace
As I walked, I embraced the beauty of solitude
Finding strength within myself and my own peace.

Though we'll never walk together side by side
Let me cherish the memories forever held dear
For in this snowy landscape I find solace
A bittersweet reminder of love once near.

And so I continue along this snow-covered path
With each step I heal, I grow, I atone,
For as I walk alone embracing the unknown
I discover a strength within me I've never known.

WHISPER IN THE WIND

There was a whisper in the wind
A gentle murmur, soothing hymn
"You are healing," it softly said
As it danced among the trees overhead.

"You are loved," the whisper declared
A message of warmth that filled the air
It wrapped around the weary soul
Embracing wounds making them whole.

"You are further ahead on your journey than you know"
The wind's voice carried with a gentle flow
It spoke of progress, of steps taken,
Of growth, of strengths, of lessons awakened.

And as the whisper lingered near
It whispered secrets only hearts could hear
"You are beginning to attract
The abundance you deserve in life's grand act."

It spoke of dreams that would unfold
Of blessings yet to be bestowed
It whispered of hope of endless possibility
Revealing a future filled with prosperity.

The whisper in the wind; it spoke with grace
A symphony of words, an embrace
It whispered of love, of healing, of worth
Filling the vast expanse of this earth

So listen closely to the whisper in the wind
Let it guide you on the path you've been
In its message, the truth reveals
That you are cherished beyond what time conceals

Embrace the abundance that's drawn near
Let it wash away every doubt, every fear
For the whisper in the wind has broken
You are meant for greatness unbroken.

NOTHING COMES FROM NOTHING

In a song they say,
"Nothing comes from Nothing
And Nothing ever will,"
But if you have nothing
Can nothing be gained?

In the realm of paradox
Where emptiness and abundance collide
A dance of possibility unfolds
Within the realm of the mind.

For what is nothing but a void
A canvas waiting to be filled
A blank page yearning for words
A silence eager for sound.

From nothing springs creation
In the depths of human imagination
Ideas take shape, dreams ignite
As the seeds of potential ingnite.

From nothing passion emerges
A fire that burns with fervor
Igniting the spark of innovation
That propels us forward.

From nothing love blossoms
A gentle whisper in the wind
A connection that knows no bounds
As hearts intertwine and mend.

From nothing strength arises
A phoenix from the ashes
Resilience forged through trials
As we rise above life's clashes.

So heed not the song's decree
That nothing yields nothingness
For in the void miracles reside
And from nothing greatness is blissed.

Embrace the power of nothing
Let it inspire and ignite
For in the depths of nothingness
Lies the potential to take flight.

GRIEF

In the realm of grief where shadows dance
Lies a tale of loss, a mournful trace
A husband, a father, a grandfather true,
A son, and a brother bids this world adieu.

The ache of absence grips their hearts tight
As darkness descends veiling joy with blight
Through tear-filled eyes and heavy sighs
The weight of sorrow no one denies.

The laugher once shared the warmth of embrace
Now memories linger a bittersweet tace
The echoes of love now whispered in pain
For loss knows no bounds, no mercy to feign.

The days turn cloudy, emotions collide
Yet, through the gloom a flicker abides
For in the depths of sorrow's cruel hold
A glimmer of hope, a story unfolds,

The sun will rise with its golden light
Chasing away the anguish of the night
Though scars remain, etches deep within
Life's resolute spirit begins to begin.

In cherished memories their spirits reside
Leading and comforting, a gentle guide
Their love unbroken, forever alive
In the hearts of those who strove to survive.

The sadness of loss, a burden to bear
Yet strength emerges from depths of despair
As time moves forward, healing will grow
And with each passing day new strength will show

Through tender moments and solace sought
The sun will shine again casting away bad thoughts
In the embrace of love we find our way
Honoring those we've lost day by day

So let the tears fall, let grief have its say
For it is in mourning that healing will sway
In the depths of loss we'll somehow find
The strength to carry on, to leave no love behind.

SNOW SNOW SNOW

Snow falling to the earth
Gently, gracefully a winter's rebirth
Each delicate flake unique and pure
Transforming the world a tranquil allure

Children frolic, their spirits alight
In this ethereal world so crisp and bright
With nimble fingers and hearts full of glee
They sculpt snowmen as jolly as can be

Snow angels aplenty, imprinted with care
Whispers of innocence filling the air
Their laughter echoes like tinkling chimes
A symphony of joy frozen in time

Footprints dance upon the snowy ground
A testament to moments so profound
Every step a story left behind
Of friendship forged, memories enshrined

Snow snow snow
Nature's gift, nature's snow
A winter wonderland pure and true
A canvas for dreams to bloom and accrue

So let the snowflakes continue to fall
Blanketing the world, enchanting all
For in this snowy tapestry we find
A haven of laughter, love intertwined

Snow snow snow
Timeless magic don't you know?
Let's savor these moments, let them flow
For in the snow our spirits forever glow.

A HAND TO HOLD

A hand to hold, a gentle touch,
In moments when life feels too much
It's comforting, a soothing balm.
As we drift into slumber's calm.

The feeling of being loved,
A warmth that cannot be shoved,
It fills our hearts, it sets us free,
As we surrender to sweet dreams' decree.

For in the moment, all is right,
As we hold on to love's pure light.
It's a win, a victory won
In this world where battles are never done.

But when the hand is gone
And we wake up to face the dawn
There's a feeling of emptiness–
A void that's hard to suppress.

Yet we rise, we carry on,
With the hope that love will dawn
In every new day that we face
We find the strength to embrace.

The memories of that hand to hold,
The love that once made us bold
And though it may be gone from sight,
It still guides us through the darkest night.

So let us cherish every hand we hold,
For in this journey, they are our gold,
And even when they may depart.
Love remains, a beating heart.

DAMN YOU, DAMN YOU

Damn you, Damn you, why do you have this hold
On my heart, it's a feeling I can't control?
Is it your smile, so warm and bright,
That makes me feel like everything will be alright?

Or perhaps it's your eyes, deep and true,
They see through my walls, they see the real me too,
They captivate me, leaving me powerless,
I can't escape, I'm in this love's harness.

Your kind nature, it's like a soothing balm
In a world that can be so cruel and calm
You show me kindness, in every single way
And it's something I cannot seem to push away.

Damn you, Damn you, for making me feel,
For stirring emotions that I thought were unreal
You've opened my heart, and I can't turn back
I'm falling for you, in every single track.

But damn you, damn you, for not feeling the same
For not reciprocating, for not playing this game,
My heart cannot let you go, it's holding on tight,
To the hope that one day, you'll see the light.

So damn you, damn you, for having this pull
On my heart, it's a love that's so full,
I'll keep on loving, even if it's in vain
Because for you, my heart will always remain.

NOT THE PRETTIEST

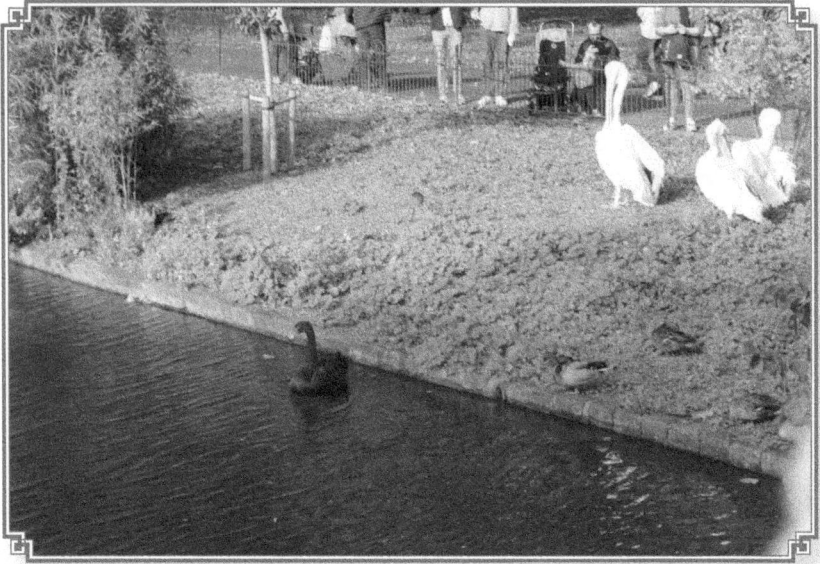

I am not the prettiest, it's true
But my worth is not defined by societal views,
I may not be a great beauty, they say,
But I am so much more than what meets the eye today.

For I am blessed by what I have been allowed
A heart that loves, a soul that's good,
No, I am not a genius, it's plain to see,
But that doesn't lessen the beauty inside of me.

I am not a rocket scientist, it is clear
But I am blessed by what I have been given
A mind to think, a heart to listen.

I am a mother, with love in my embrace
I am a daughter, with a smile on my face
I am a sister, a friend through and through
And I am blessed by the bonds that hold me true.

I may not fit society's ideal
But I'm blessed with a love that is real.
I may not be perfect, but I am enough
For I am blessed with a heart that's tough.

So let them say what say what they will,
I am content with my blessings still
For I know who I am, and that's enough
For I am blessed with a life that's filled with love.

HELLO DARLING

We are strong to survive
Through every trial and strife
With a special connection
That no one else can describe.

Though sometimes it's hard to see
The light at the end of the road
We hold on tight, hand in hand
Together, we'll bear the load.

I remember the day
When I longed for something true
I held my breath, closed my eyes
And then I saw you

You were there in front of me
A dream come to life
And my breathe caught in my heart
As you said, "Hello Darling,"

With just two words
You took my heart by storm
And I knew right then and there
We were meant to be born.

Through every trial and strife
We'll stand side be side
For we are strong to survive
With you, I have nothing to hide.

MEME LUKWITZ-MIHALOVIC

We have a special connection
That no one can understand
But that's what makes it so beautiful
Our love is one of a kind.

So let's hold on tight
And face the world together
For our love is a beacon
That will shine forever.

Yes, we are strong to survive
Through every hardship and pain
With each other by our side
We'll endure and we'll remain.

And every time you say,
"Hello Darling," with your smile
I'll know without a doubt
Together, we can conquer any trial.

I AM...

I am a mother, nurturing and kind
With a love that knows no bounds
My children are my heart and soul
A love that forever astounds.

I am a daughter, with a bond so strong,
To my mother, my guiding light
She taught me to be brave and bold
And to always stand up for what is right.

I am a sister, a friend for life
Through thick and thin, we stand by each other
Together we laugh, together we cry
A bond that will never wither.

But I am more than these roles I play
I am my own person, unique and true
I am more than just a title
I am me, and that's enough, it is true.

I am a reader, escaping to other worlds
Through the pages of a book
I am a writer, creating my own reality
With every word, I can change and look.

I am strong with a heart of fire
I have faced challenges and pain
But I rise above, with my head held high
And I won't let anyone dim my flame.

I am wise, with lessons learned
From every experience, I grow
I am a woman, confident and fierce
With a spirit that continues to glow.

I am invincible, nothing can break me
For I have a heart of steel
I am a warrior, fighting every battle
With grace, strength, and a love that's real.

I have paid the price, for my dreams and goals
But I will never give up on my fight
For I have a long way to go
And I will continue to shine bright.

And through it all I have love to give
To my family, my friends, and to you
For I am a mother, daughter, a sister
But most of all, I am me, and that's true.

MY COUSIN

My cousin
My sister
My protector
Each one holds a special place in my heart.
We've shared laughs and tears
Through the passing years,
And our bond grows stronger with every start.

My cousin, dear
With your infectious smile
You light up any room you're in,
Though miles may separate us
Our love remains strong
And through thick and thin, we'll always win.

My sister, my rock,
You've always been there
Through the ups and downs of life.
With you unwavering support
And your loving embrace
I know I can conquer any strife.

My protector, my shield
You've always had my back
Through battles both big and small.
With your courage and strength
I've learned to be brave
And stand tall through it all.

MEME LUKWITZ-MIHALOVIC

Together we've grown
Through sunshine and rain
With each other we've found comfort and love.
No matter where life takes us
We'll always be family
Held together by an unbreakable bond from above.

So here's to my cousin
My sister, my protector
My heart is forever yours.
Through all of life's journey
We'll always stand together
And our love will continue to soar.

LOVE MEANS

Love means so many different things to people.
It's a tapestry woven with threads of complexity.
A symphony of emotions, a kaleidoscope of forms.

Love, the enigmatic force that defies definition.
An ever-changing chameleon, adapting to each heart's desire.
It whispers sweet nothings in the quiet of a moonlit night,
And screams its presence in the raging storms of passion.

Love, the gentle touch that heals wounds unseen.
A soothing balm for the scars that life has inflicted.
It nurtures, it comforts, it holds us in its embrace,
Guiding through the darkest of nights, lighting our way.

Love, the fierce protector of fragile hearts,
A warrior standing tall against the tides of adversity.
It fuels the fires of courage, ignites the flames of hope,
And shields us from the arrows of doubt and despair.

Love, the unspoken language that binds souls,
An invisible thread connecting us across distance and time.
It speaks through a smile, a glance, a gentle caress,
And dances in the spaces between our interlinked fingers.

Love, the wild untamed spirit that sets hearts ablaze,
A tempest of emotions that knows no bounds.
It is the ecstasy of a stolen kiss, the ache of a longing heart,
And the serenity found in the depths of a lover's gaze.

Love means so many different things to people,
For it is a vast sea with endless depths to explore
It is the essence of our existence, the very fabric of life,
In all its forms, in all its emotions, love is ours to cherish.

MEME LUKWITZ-MIHALOVIC

LINGUISTIC

In this linguistic dance, we twirl
You say arse, I say ass, our words unfurl,
A tapestry woven with different threads,
Yet, understanding blooms in our shared threads.

You call them mates, those dear to your heart,
While I prefer friends, a bond from the start,
Language may differ, but meanings align,
For companionship transcends any design.

You dream of holidays, a time to unwind,
While I crave vacations, a respite to find,
Through different words, we see the same release,
A break from the mundane, a moment of peace.

You indulge in biscuits, a savory treat,
But I enjoy cookies, their sweetness complete,
A simple delight satisfying and true,
In our varied tongues, joy finds its debut.

And when it comes to pudding, a culinary delight,
you relish its richness, a taste that ignites,
but I prefer dessert, a spectrum so vast,
a world of flavors, from future to past.

So let us embrace these linguistic shades,
For in our differences, beauty cascades,
We may speak distinct, but our essence entwines,
In the tapestry of words, a harmony shines.

AN OCEAN APART

Just an ocean between us
Friends from afar,
You are a storyteller
Where I am poet.

In this vast expanse of water
Our connection remains unbroken
Through words and tales
We bridge the distance, unspoken.

Your stories dance like waves
Crashing onto distant shores
While my verses softly whisper
In the winds that gently soar.

MEME LUKWITZ-MIHALOVIC

You weave intricate plots,
Characters with lives untold
I paint emotions with words,
Colors of love, sorrow, and bold.

Though we reside in different realms,
Our hearts beat as one
Through ink and paper, we unite,
A friendship that's never undone.

Just an ocean between us,
Yet, our souls intertwine
We're poets in different forms,
Creating beauty, divine.

So let the waves carry our voices,
Across this vast and endless sea
For though we may be apart
Forever friends, we'll always be.

WAS THERE A SPARK

Was there a spark?
No, but there was an ember.
A flickering light in the depths of my soul
A gentle warmth, a glimmer of hope.

Were my dreams of you exaggerated?
No, because the person who was in front of me
Was so much better than my dreams.
You surpassed every expectation, it seems.

In the shadows of my mind, I had woven a tale
Of a love so grand, a love that would prevail
But reality, oh reality, you proved me wrong,
For what stood before me was a love so strong.

Your presence, a symphony of grace and charm
Each word you spoke, a soothing balm,
Your eyes, windows to a world unknown
Revealing depths of compassion I had never known.

In your laughter, a melody danced on the air,
A sound so sweet, banishing all despair
Your touch, a gentle caress, igniting my skin
Sending shivers down my spine, from deep within.

No, there was no spark, but an ember so bright
A slow burn, growing steadily in the night
And as it flickered and danced, I realized
That this ember had the power to mesmerize.

MEME LUKWITZ-MIHALOVIC

With each passing moment, our love took flight
Igniting a fire, burning ever so bright
And though it started as a mere ember's glow
It blossomed into a love that continues to grow.

So, let the flames rise, let them reach the sky
For in your arms, I've found my reasons why
No, there was no spark, but an ember so true
And in this love, I've found my forever with you.

A SONNET - MORNING HAS BROKEN

They say the sky is bright with hues of purples, oranges, and pinks
A tapestry of colors woven by the dawn's gentle hand
As morning awakens, nature's canvas softly winks
Revealing a masterpiece, divinely planned.

White clouds painting the sky, strokes so pure and light,
Whispering secrets, floating with graceful ease,
Day has broken, a symphony of radiant might,
A glorious blue expanse, where dreams find their release.

Big billowing clouds with the sun's warm embrace,
Unfolding like petals, reaching for the heavens above,
Providing us its warmth, a tender, loving grace.
A celestial dance, an eternal pledge of love.

Evening has descended upon us, its colors ablaze,
With the setting sun casting reds, yellows, and ambers,
A golden farewell, as twilight's curtain begins to raise,
Whispering lullabies, as daylight surrenders.

Night has fallen, a canopy of inky black
Dripping with stars, like diamonds on velvet display
A celestial tapestry, weaving dreams and hope back,
Guiding our soul through darkness, lighting our way.

Morning has broken, day and night entwined,
Nature's symphony, a timeless work of art,
In this eternal dance, our spirits aligned,
Finding solace and beauty, a healing impart.

So let us embrace each dawn and twilight's glow
In the vast expanse of life's ever-changing scene
For in the colors that paint our world and flow
We find solace, joy, and the love that lies between.

This sonnet, a tribute to nature's grand design
With words that strive to capture its grandeur
In this large-sized verse, may your spirit align
With the beauty that surrounds, forever to endure.

LANGUAGE AND EXPRESSION

In this vast world of language and expression,
Where meaning intertwines with each confession,
To me, a torch is a flashlight, shining bright,
Guiding my steps through the darkest of night.

A mate, to me, is a cherished, loyal friend,
Whose presence brings comfort till the very end,
A garden, for me, is the backyard's embrace,
Where nature's beauty dances with tranquil grace.

A biscuit, to me, is a sweet, delectable treat,
A cookie that makes my taste buds dance and greet,
While a jumper is a cozy sweater,
Wrapping me in warmth in cold winter weather.

Yet amidst these differences, we find a way
To bridge the gaps, and our hearts convey,
For we both say "Love" with the very same voice,
A word that unites, a choice that we rejoice.

In the language of the soul, love knows no divide,
It binds us together, side by side,
Across cultures and tongues, it stays constant and true,
A universal emotion, for me and for you.

MEME LUKWITZ-MIHALOVIC

So let us celebrate the beauty we share,
In the words we use, unique and rare,
For though meaning may vary, and words may change,
Love's essence remains, eternally in range.

So, to me, a torch is a flashlight's gleam,
A mate is a friend, a garden, a dream,
And though a biscuit may be a cookie to me,
We both say "Love" in perfect harmony.

YOU SCARE ME

You scare me
With your enigmatic allure,
Yet, we could talk about anything,
Dive into the depth of our souls,
Unearthing secrets and dreams.

You are someone
So vastly different from me,
Universe of complexities,
And I, a mere wanderer,
But when I see you smile,
When your eyes laugh with pure delight,
I feel the magnetic pull,
The center of your universe.

In your presence, time expands,
The world fades away,
Leaving only you and me,
Lost in a moment of serendipity.
Your laughter, like a symphony,
Fills the air with melodies divine,
And I, a captive audience,
Mesmerized by your light.

You scare me,
For I am but a simple sort,
A yearning for the unknown,
A craving for the extraordinary,
In your presence, I am transformed,
Unleashing the essence of my being,
Exploring the uncharted territories,
Becoming more than ever thought possible.

MEME LUKWITZ-MIHALOVIC

You scare me,
But in that fear lies exhilaration,
A dance on the edge of uncertainty,
For you are the catalyst,
The catalyst of growth and self-discovery.
Together we embark on a journey,
Where words become our compass,
And vulnerability our guide,
In this vast universe we create.

You scare me,
And I embrace that fear,
For within it lies the magic,
The magic of connection,
Of findng solace in the unfamiliar,
Of unraveling the tapestry of your soul,
And intertwining it with mine,

In a symphony of cosmic harmony.
You scare me,
Yet I am drawn to you,
Like a moth to a flame,
For in your presence,
I find a reflection of my own essence.
A reminder that we are all connected,
That our differences are what make us beautiful,
And that, together, we can conquer the universe.

WANDERING MIND

Why does the mind wander
In meandering paths unknown,
Through a labyrinth of thoughts,
Unfolding like a river's flow?

Why won't the mind shut down,
A ceaseless symphony of noise,
Whispers of forgotten dreams,
Echoing in restless poise?

Why can't I get my story out,
Words tangled in a web of doubt,
A tale imprisoned in my core,
Yearning to break free, to shout?

Oh, the mind, a wild beast it seems,
Roaming freely in boundless realms
Seeking solace, seeking truth
In the depths of its infinite helms.

But fear not, oh restless soul,
For within this chaos lies a key,
Unlock the floodgates of your mind,
And set your story, your spirit, free.

MISSING YOU

Missing you,
Do you miss me?
Is there a future?
Will there always be space between us?

These questions echo in my mind,
Whispering softly in the quiet of night,
The longing, the ache,
It consumes me, day and night.

I yearn for your touch,
The warmth of your embrace.
But distance separates us,
Leaving only empty space.

Will time bring us closer,
Or push us further apart?
Uncertainty lingers,
Tugging at my fragile heart.

In this vast expanse,
I search for sign,
A glimmer of hope,
That our love will align.

Yet, through it all,
I hold onto the belief,
That destiny will unite us,
And bring solace to my grief.

Missing you,
Do you miss me too?
In the vastness of this world,
I'll wait, hoping our love will come through.

ASHES TO ASHES

Ashes to ashes,
Dust to dust,
Is that what our lives come down to?
For the loved ones we have left behind?

In this fleeting existence,
Where moments slip through our grasp,
We find solace in the memories
Of those who have passed.

Their laughter echoes in our hearts,
Their touch still lingers in the air,
Though they have departed,
Their love remains ever fair.

For in the realm of the eternal,
Their spirits dance and soar,
Guiding us through life's journey,
Forever, and even more.

Gone from our sight,
Yet forever in our souls,
Their presence, a gentle whisper,
That softly consoles.

So let us not mourn
With sorrow's heavy weight,
But celebrate their lives,
Embrace their love innate.

For as the ashes settle,
And the dust settles too,
Their essence lives on
In everything we do.

In every breath we take,
In every tear we shed,
Their memory intertwines
With the stories we spread.

Ashes to ashes,
Dust to dust,
But love, ah love, it never dies,
For it's the legacy we trust.

MEME LUKWITZ-MIHALOVIC

IS THERE LIFE AFTER DEATH?

Is there life after death?
Does grief let us move on?
Or does grief hold us back?

In this vast universe of unknowns,
We ponder the great mysteries,
Seeking solace, seeking truth.

The heart aches, the soul weeps,
A glimmer of home begins to stir,
A whisper of something beyond.

For grief may bind us, keep us tethered,
To memories and moments cherished,
But it is not our eternal captor.

In the depth of sorrow's embrace,
We find strength, we find resilience,
And the courage to forge ahead.

For life after death may not be tangible,
But the spirit of those we've lost,
Lives on in the tapestry of our being.

They become the stars that guide us,
The gentle breeze that caresses our cheek,
The whispered words that fill our dreams.

So, let grief be the catalyst for growth,
The fuel that ignites our inner flame,
As we navigate this journey called life.

And though we may stumble and falter,
In the face of grief's relentless grip,
We will rise, we will endure.

For in the depths of sorrow's embrace,
We find the strength to carry on,
Discovering that life after death is love.

MEME LUKWITZ-MIHALOVIC

WORLD AUTISM AWARENESS MONTH

How do you love a person on the spectrum?
Very simply, they are the way God made them.
Acceptance and Compassion
In this month of awareness and understanding,
Let us embrace the beauty of diversity,
And celebrate the unique gifts and perspectives
That those on the spectrum bring to the world.
Love them for who they are,
For their quirks and their passions,
For the way they see the world,
In colors and patterns we may never know.
Let us extend a hand of kindness,
And walk alongside them with patience,
For they are not broken, but whole,
In their own magnificent way.
Let us listen to their voices,
And learn from their wisdom,
For they have much to teach us
About love, acceptance, and compassion.
So let us stand together,
In solidarity and support,
For those on the spectrum,
They are truly a gift from above.

DAMNATION'S EMBRACE

Oh. Damn thee for thy siren's call,
That voice that echoes through my soul,
With every word, my senses all,
Ensnared within thy sweet control.

Thine eyes, like stars, ignite with fire,
Thy gaze intoxicate my mind,
In thy depths, I lose desire,
Beguiled by thy celestial kind.

Thy smile, a radiant morning's beam,
Warms my heart and sets me ablaze,
A laughter that weaves a vibrant dream,
Casting its magic through my maze.

But most of all, thy face I fear,
For in its lines, I find my fate,
A tapestry of beauty, clear,
Where I am forever lost and great.

ECHOES OF THE PAST

A spark, a word, ignite a flame,
Reviving memories, a nostalgic flame.
A voice, like echoes from a distant past,
Brings forth a face, a love that long did last.

A flicker on the screen, a memory's dance,
A childhood's joy, a heart's sweet trance.
An actor's guise, a visage in the night,
Awakens dreams, a love once bright.

A book's embrace, a sanctuary of words,
Recalls the thrill that ignites love's chords.
A tale unravels, a writer's might,
Unleashing inspiration day and night.

But ever-present, like a guiding light,
That spark of conversation, a beacon of insight.
It bridges time and space, a tapestry entwined,
Connecting fragments, memories intertwined.

In childhood's echoes and in love's embers,
That spark of talk reveals a timeless grace.
For in its warmth, the past and present blend,
A symphony of love, where hearts transcend.

THE SOUND OF SILENCE

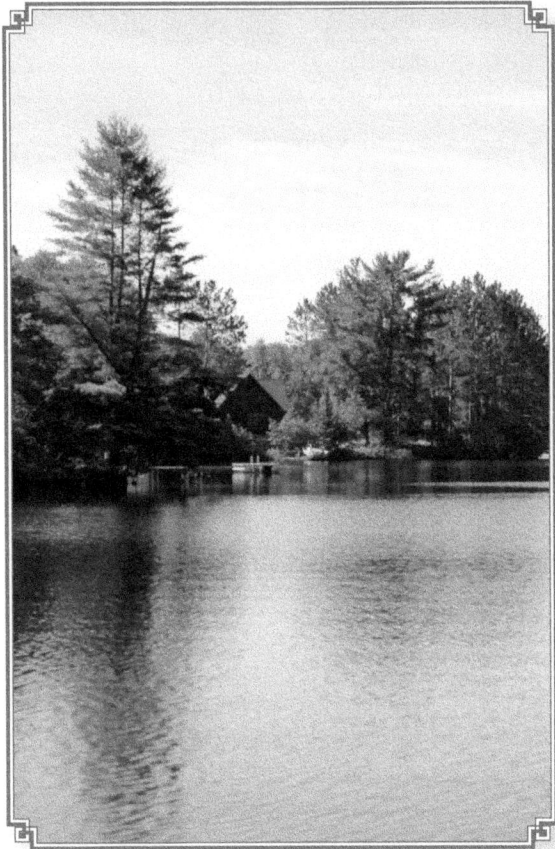

In depths of silence, where no sound pervades,
A symphony of thoughts the mind invades.
Like rivers flowing, imagination streams,
Unveiling worlds beyond our waking dreams.

No rustling leaves or crashing waves to heed.
In this ethereal calm, the soul is freed.
A canvas void, where reveries ignite,
A tapestry of visions, pure and bright.

The humming silence stills the restless mind,
No fridge's drone, no flickering lights to find.
The TV's void allows the soul to soar,
To realms unknown, where secrets lie in store.

The silence, a celestial call,
Inviting contemplation, answering life's call.
For in the quiet, truth resides new,
A sanctuary for thoughts, both old and new.

TORN HEART'S CRY

'Fuck you,' my tongue rebels in vain,
While my heart whispers, 'Fuck me again.'
The hold you have, a cruel embrace,
A prison where my thoughts find no space.

'Let it go,' my mind implores,
But the heart's desire, it cannot ignore.
Even in reason's cold embrace,
Love's flame burns bright, demanding its place.

The battle rages within my soul,
A chasm between passion and control.
I yearn to break free, to shed your sway,
But the chains of affection hold me at bay.

'Fuck me,' my heart pleads, filled with despair,
As I submit to its relentless prayer.
The pain, the heartache, I willingly bear,
For in its depths, I find a perverse care.

'Fuck you,' I say, but my words ring hollow,
For the heart's desires reign supreme, I follow.
Trapped in as cycle of love and hate,
I surrender to my bittersweet fate.

MEME LUKWITZ-MIHALOVIC

WITH YOU

With you, my dear, I soar to heights,
Unreachable by me alone,
You ignite within me boundless might,
Making dreams feel close to home.

We conquer fears, a formidable foe,
With you, I find the strength I lack.
Your presence calms my anxious flow,
A sanctuary where I can't be attached.

Your love envelops me like a warm embrace,
A haven where my worries fade,
With you, I find a safe and tranquil space,
A sanctuary where love's flames cascade.

For in your love, I find steadfast guide,
A beacon that dispels the darkest night.
With you, my dear, there's nothing we can't stride,
For your love empowers me to take flight.

So let us venture forth, hand in hand,
With you, my fear is calmed, my spirit bold.
Together, we will conquer any land,
As your love makes all things seem old.

YESTERDAY'S SORROW

Yesterday's sorrows, a distant haze,
Dispersed by time's relentless gaze.
The pain subsides, the wounds begin to heal.
As hope's tender tendrils gently steal.

Only tomorrow lies ahead, unknown,
A tapestry of joy and pain yet to be sown.
Uncertainty looms large, a haunting specter,
But within its folds, hidden seeds of nectar.

Gloomy skies above, a somber shroud,
Yet through the clouds, a silver lining bowed.
For in the darkest nights, stars find their way,
Guiding hearts to a brighter day.

So let us shed the weight of yesterday's woes,
And embrace the promise that tomorrow holds.
With open hearts and spirits yet unbowed,
We'll force a path towards dreams yet loud.

MEME LUKWITZ-MIHALOVIC

MY BROTHER, MY BASTION

In our kin's embrace, youngest thou art,
My guardian, my playmate, a joy to my heart.
Shoulder to lean on, a being so true,
My brother, unwavering, my solace for you.

'Baby brother,' I tease with a grin,
Yet deep within I know what you've always been.
A protector, a playmate, a friend though and through,
Your presence a treasure, wherever I go.

Through life's ups and downs, we've stood side by side,
Your laughter my beacon, my worries you'd hide.
From childhood's antics to adulthood's cares,
Your unwavering bond has eased all my fears.

Your shoulder, a refuge, a place of repose,
Where I can confide my dreams, my joys, and my woes.
You listen with patience, offer wise counsel,
Guiding my path, keeping me from derail.

May our bond forever remain strong and true,
My brother, my bastion, my unwavering clue.
For in your presence, I find solace and might,
A constant companion, a light in the night.

PRIMROSE HILL'S EMBRACE

On Primrose Hill, where heights ascend,
A vista grand, the soul does mend.
At dawn's embrace, or twilight's kiss,
A symphony of colors, a breathtaking bliss.

The crimson sky, a fiery hue,
As morning paints the canvas anew.
The golden orb, a beacon bright,
Illuminating heavens with its light.

As evening falls, the colors shift,
From amber gold to hues that drift.
The setting sun, a radiant glow,
Painting the skyline with a vibrant show.

From London's rooftops, far and wide,
The view unfolds a city's pride.
St. Paul's golden dome, the Tower's crest,
A tapestry of landmarks, truly blessed.

Beneath the gentle breeze that whispers by,
The city's hum, a distant lullaby.
Primrose Hill, a sanctuary of peace,
Where worries fade, and spirits find release.

So climb the slope, embrace the view,
Let nature's wonders your soul imbue.
From sunrise's birth to sunset's fall,
Primrose Hill's magic captivates all.

MEME LUKWITZ-MIHALOVIC

BRIGHTON'S WEST PIER

In Brighton's waters stands a sight,
A living canvas, day and night.
The West Pier, a skeletal embrace,
A masterpiece of time and space.

Birds alight upon its rusty frame,
A symphony of life amidst the flame.
Sunrise hues and sunset's glow
Paint the pier with vibrant flow.

Black and ash, a somber shell,
Reflecting colors it once held.
Yet, through the gloom, a spirit gleams,
A testament to art's enduring dreams.

As eerie fog enwraps its form,
The pier becomes a realm of storm.
Mystery shrouds its ancient core,
A haunting presence, evermore.

But still it breathes, a living art,
Connecting past and present, heart to heart.
In Brighton's soul, it holds its place,
A timeless treasure, full of grace.

A MOTHER DAUGHTER TRIP

In London's embrace, they wandered free,
A mother and daughter, hand in hand,
Through bustling streets and ancient lanes,
Their hearts alight with a shared delight.

They ventured forth with eager steps,
Exploring a city steeped in tales,
Where history whispered from every stone,
And dreams took flight in the city's haze.

From Buckingham Palace to the Tower Bridge,
They marveled at grandeur and architectural grace,
The Thames flowed beneath their gaze,
A ribbon of life, forever in motion.

In Covent Garden, they danced with glee
To street performers, their spirits set free,
Laughter echoed through the vibrant square,
A symphony of joy, filling the air.

Museums and galleries held treasures untold,
Art and artifacts, stories of old,
They stood in awe, eyes filled with wonder,
Immersed in culture, their souls grew fonder.

The West End stage beckoned in lights,
Musicals and plays, magical nights,
They sat in hushed anticipation
As performances unfolded in pure elation.

But amidst the chaos of this great city,
They found solace in quiet corners,
A park bench beneath a blooming tree,
A moment of peace, just the two of them.

As the days unfolded, so did their bond,
A tapestry woven with love and care,
Through conversations and shared experiences,
A mother and daughter, a lifelong affair.

And when their time in London drew to an end,
Their memories etched upon their hearts,
But a connection that would never depart.

For in the streets of London, they discovered
That the truest treasure of all
Was the gift of time shared together,
A mother and daughter standing tall.

PARIS, WHERE DREAMS DANCE

In Paris, where dreams dance upon cobblestone streets,
A mother and daughter embarked on a journey sweet,
Hand in hand they wandered through the city of lights
With hearts alight and spirits taking flight.

Eiffel Tower stood tall, kissing the sky above,
As they marveled at its elegance, so full of love.
They climbed its iron stairs, step by step,
Breathing in the beauty, no words to intercept

The Louvre beckoned, with its treasures untold,
Whispering secrets of artists, both young and old.
Mother and daughter stood before Mona Lisa's smile
Captivated by her enigmatic, timeless guile.

Down the Seine, their laughter filled the air,
As they sailed upon the river without a care.
Bridges whispered stories, whispered tales
Of lovers entwined and ships setting sail.

Montmartre's streets were alive with vibrant hues,
Painters capturing moments, refusing to lose.
Hand in hand, they climbed the winding hill,
To Sacre-Coeur where their hearts stood still.

And in cozy cafes, they savored each bite,
Indulging in croissants under the soft moonlight.
Conversations flowed, like the river's gentle stream,
Mother and daughter sharing secrets, as in a dream.

But time, relentless, tugged at their embrace,
As their Parisian adventure reached its final space.
They bid farewell to the city with bittersweet sighs,
Leaving behind memories, in their hearts, to rise.

For in Paris, their bond grew stronger, unfurled,
A mother and daughter exploring the world.
United by love in a city so rare,
Their trip to Paris, a memory they'll forever share.

So, they return home, carrying Paris with them,
Forever grateful for the journey where love did begin.
And as life unfolds, they'll forever reminisce
The mother and daughter trip to Paris, pure bliss.

THE CITY

The city that I consider heaven
Is full of magic to behold.
It doesn't matter your skin color,
This place will make you feel alive.

The canals are lined with pleasure boats,
Museums open their doors.
Fountains in the parks,
Statues of the past,
All there to explore.

The smell of fresh cut grass,
Trees lined up in rows.
The sound of children playing
In gardens, paths, and rows.

In this city, you can breathe,
The energy is everywhere.
People who live here
Love this place and take in the air.

This city, of which I speak,
Is heaven, I believe.
It's full of life and moments
Where dreams can be achieved and explored.

THE FOG

The fog has lifted,
A light that brings clarity,
Concepts that have been obsure,
Now become clear to me.

Once confusion, now understanding,
My thoughts become clear,
Where there was doubt, now conviction,
My faith I will not fear.

The fog has lifted,
My sight has grown so much more,
My thoughts now become more precise,
My goals I do explore.

The fog has lifted,
My vision is now so clear,
My path is now so certain,
My faith I will not fear.

MEME LUKWITZ-MIHALOVIC

THE BOARDWALK

I walk along the boardwalk in the rain,
Searching for rainbows, my woes to assuage.
The rain slowly dampening my everyday pain,
Making memories of all the happy days.

The sky is a grey blanket above me,
The sun nowhere to be seen.
But I still look for rainbows,
Not defeated, for I have hope.

In a silver lining, I see glimpse of color,
Dancing along the wind-tossed waves.
It streaks the sky with a mote of happiness,
Reassurance from God no matter the days.

The sea is a dark abyss below me,
Where the sun's might cannot reach.
But when I look for rainbows this time,
New beauty springs out of the depths.

I walk along the boardwalk in the rain,
Making memories of the present and past.
Though the grey sky hides the sun's flame,
I keep looking for rainbows, never aghast.

DEPTHS OF NIGHT

In the depths of night, where shadows play,
The moonlight dances upon the bay,
A shimmering path upon the sea,
Inviting us to set our spirits free.

Beneath the stars a gentle lullaby,
Whispers of secrets, no need to pry,
The world is still as darkness surrounds,
Yet in his moment, tranquility is abound.

Hand in hand, we venture to the shore,
Where moonbeams paint the waves galore,
Like liquid silver they caress our skin,
As we surrender to the moonlight's whims.

With each step, the water kisses our toes,
A symphony of ripples, as the ocean flows,
Silent whispers of the night call to us,
Guiding us towards a surreal chorus.

We dive into the depths, as one we glide,
In this moonlit realm, where dreams reside,
Weightless, we float, our bodies entwined,
Lost in the beauty of this celestial find.

As the moonlight bathes our souls with grace,
We become one with the night's embrace.
For in this moment, we are truly free,
Under the moon's watchful eye, you and me.

MEME LUKWITZ-MIHALOVIC

In this moonlight swim, where time stands skill,
We find solace in the calmness, the thrill,
Unburdened hearts, as we let go,
In this mystical dance, our spirits grow.

So let us forever chase the moon's glow
In this moonlight swim, together we'll go,
For in its luminous glow, we find our bliss,
In the moonlight's caress, we find our kiss.

BOUND BY BLOOD

Bound by blood and love,
Two souls entwined,
By fate's hand above.

In childhood's embrace,
We laughed and we played,
Sharing secrets and dreams
In a world we had made.

Through trials and triumphs,
We stood side by side,
Supporting each other
With hearts open wide.

Different paths we chose,
Yet still we remain,
Connected by a bond
That time can't restrain.

Through distance and time,
Our connection held strong,
Though miles may separate us,
Our love carries on.

My cousin,
Forever we'll be,
Two souls intertwined,
In a bond that is free.

DAWN'S GENTLE LIGHT

In the dawn's gentle light, a bond is formed,
A mother's love, a daughter's heart adorned,
They dance through life like whispers in the breeze,
Their souls entwined, a harmony of ease.

A tender touch, a guiding hand,
In moments of joy and times unplanned.
Through laughter and tears, they navigate the years,
Bridging the gaps, dispelling all fears.

Each step they take side by side,
A shared journey, where love resides,
In their glances, secrets softly exchanged,
A language unspoken, emotions arranged.

The mother, a beacon of strength and grace,
Nurturing her daughter's dreams leaving no trace,
She teaches her resilience, lessons untold,
Empowering her to be fearless and bold.

The daughter, a reflection, a mirror so true,
Absorbing wisdom, like morning's dew,
She learns from her mother, her guiding light,
Growing in her presence, reaching new heights.

Through the seasons, their bond remains,
A tapestry woven with love's gentle reins,
In moments of triumph, they cheer and embrace,
In times of sorrow, they find solace and grace.

For in this dance, they find their way,
A mother and daughter, come what may,
Their love unbreakable, a cherished treasure,
A bond that defies time's fleeting measure.

So, let their story forever unfold,
In the hearts of mothers and daughters untold,
For their connection, an everlasting flame,
A testament to love's enduring claim.

A BOND IS FORMED

In the depths of love, a bond is formed.
A sacred connection, where hearts are warmed.
A mother and son, an unbreakable tie,
Through laughter and tears, they soar high.

She cradles him gently, with arms so strong,
Nurturing his spirit, where he belongs,
Her touch, a soft whisper, a comforting grace,
Guiding him through life's unpredictable maze.

She's his shelter, his haven, when skies turn gray,
A steady compass, showing him the way.
With each step he takes, she's by his side,
Holding his hand, as they journey with pride.

In her eyes, he sees a reflection of self,
A mirror of love, that transcends all wealth.
He learns from her wisdom, imbibes her grace,
Her spirit, a beacon, in life's hectic race.

From childhood to manhood they evolve and grow,
Their bond deepens, as time continues to flow.
He's her pride, her joy, her reason to be,
She treasures each moment, for eternity.

Through ups and downs, their love remains true,
A bond unbreakable, forever in view,
For in the tapestry of life, they are woven,
A mother and son, a love never stolen.

In the dance of life, they twirl and spin,
A harmony so beautiful, from deep within,
The mother and son, forever connected,
A love story, pure and unaffected.

Short in size, but vast in emotion,
Their love defies any worldly notion.
A testament to the power of affection,
The mother and son, a divine connection.

MEME LUKWITZ-MIHALOVIC

THE SPIRIT OF THE DOVE

The spirit of the dove,
As breath of life anew,
Filling every heart and soul,
With love that's pure and true.

It soars through open skies
In graceful, gentle flight,
A symbol of peace and hope,
Bathing us in its light.

With wings spread wide, it brings
A sense of calm and peace,
A touch of healing grace,
That makes all worries cease.

In every whispered coo,
A melody of unity,
Uniting hearts and minds
In a bond of serenity.

The spirit of the dove,
A messenger of love's embrace,
Guiding us on a path,
Towards a better place.

So let it fill our hearts
With compassion, pure and free,
May its presence always reminds us
Of the beauty we can be.

For the spirit of the dove
Breathes new life into our being,
A gentle form of love,
Forever eternally freeing.

MEME LUKWITZ-MIHALOVIC

THE ESSENCE OF LIFE

Inhale the essence of life,
One breath at a time,
For within each precious gasp
Lives the power to revive

In this vast expanse of existence,
Where fleeting moments unwind,
Embrace the beauty of simplicity,
One minute, one hour, one day, we find.

Cast off the weights of tomorrow's worries,
Release the burdens that oppress,
For happiness resides in the present,
In the moments we eagerly possess.

In this symphony of existence,
Let each note be played with care,
For in the silence of our choices
Lives the melody we long to share.

Within every fleeting second
Lives a canvas of dreams to bloom,
Paint the colors of your desires,
And let life's possibilities consume.

With each passing hour,
Opportunity's door stands ajar.
Seize the chance to grow and learn,
To chase after your brightest star.

As the sun dances across the sky,
Illuminating each path we tread,
Embrace the light that guides you,
And let your spirit be freely led.

For happiness lies not in the destination,
But in the journey we undertake,
One step at a time, we discover
The joy that lies in our wake.

So let us breathe, let us live
In this symphony of endless time,
As with each passing moment,
May we find the happy sublime.

MEME LUKWITZ-MIHALOVIC

WHEN LIFE WAS FREE

In time of old, when life was free,
When souls were touched in harmony,
A simple act that warmed the heart,
From distance, we are now apart.

I miss the hugs that brought me peace,
Embracing love a sweet release,
The tender clutch, so warm and tight,
Now distant memories in the night.

I miss the kisses on my cheek,
Expressions of affection, unique,
Each gentle touch, a loving sign
That once upon a time were mine.

I miss the holding of your hand,
A connection that I understand,
Fingers intertwined, a bond so strong,
But now it seems forever gone.

I miss those nights, so softly shared,
Lying close, souls bared,
Discussing dreams, the highs and lows,
Creating memories, as time ebbs and flows.

Oh, how I long to feel the comfort
Of your presence, as we lay under covers,
To listen to your voice, soothing and calm,
As we navigate life's unpredictable qualm.

In absence, my heart yearns and aches,
For the warmth that only closeness makes,
But until the day when we embrace anew,
I'll hold onto hope, for love is true.

For even though we are apart,
Love's essence still resides within my heart,
And one day, when these trails transcend,
We'll share our laughter, our touch, our blend.

And so, I wait with patience pure
To feel your love's embrace once more,
For hugs and kisses, hand in hand,
Are treasures I miss in this shifting sand.

MEME LUKWITZ-MIHALOVIC

I YEARN

I miss hugs, those warm embraces so sweet,
When arms wrap 'round and sorrow retreat.
In these times of distance, I reminisce,
Of moments shared, where love did persist.

Upon my heart, a longing does reside,
For the tender touch that once did abide,
The solace found an affectionate hold,
A language unspoken, yet worth more than gold.

Life's a symphony's crescendo, they do ignite,
Filling empty spaces, bringing pure delight,
A touch, so gentle, a gentle squeeze,
Easing worries, putting my mind at ease.

With each embrace, emotions swirl and dance,
A connection deeper than circumstance,
From loved ones dear and friends so true,
Hugs have a magic that always shines through.

Oh, how I yearn for that tight squeeze,
Feeling secure, as worries do appease.
Through the power of touch, burdens subside,
And love radiates, like a rising tide.

So let us hope for days yet to come,
When we'll gather again and heal as one.
For hugs shall prevail, they'll never depart,
A testament to love's enduring art.

In absence, I've learned to cherish anew,
The beauty of hugs, and what they can do,
For when they next grace my life's embrace,
I'll hold on tightly, leaving no trace.

Until that day arrives, I'll fondly recall,
The warmth of hugs, embracing us all.
And as time marches on, bringing forth new chapters,
May hugs be the salve that heals our fractures.

DAYS LONG GONE

In days long gone, when warmth did wrap around,
A tender touch, an embrace so profound,
A gentle tango of souls entwined,
Oh, how I yearn, those moments left behind.

I miss hugs, those precious arms that held me tight,
With each squeeze, worries found their hurried flight,
A comforting haven, a sanctuary so dear,
That whispered solace, wiping away any tear.

In your embrace, worries would cease to exist,
A gentle calm, healing the heart's every twist,
In this dance of love, we found our respite,
A language unspoken, but oh what delight!

Each hug, a symphony of feeling so pure,
A sweet melody that my soul would endure,
The cadence of love in every loving squeeze,
With arms wrapped tight, we'd find perfect ease.

But now, distance keeps us apart, it seems,
An empty longing fills my tender dreams,
Yet still, I hold hope within this fragile frame
That soon, once again, I'll be held in your arms.

Through words and thoughts, I send my love anew,
Yearning for the day when our embrace is true,
For in your arms, I find my solace and peace,
Where all worries cease and emotions release.

So until the time comes for our worlds to collide,
I'll hold onto memories, with love as my guide,
Yearning for the day when our paths will align,
And once more, my dear, your love I'll enshrine.

In the meantime, I'll cherish the love that remains,
And through these words, I'll alleviate the pains,
For though I miss hugs, their power lingers still,
A testament to the love we both fulfill.

A HILL IN LONDON

At Primrose Hill, where the city sprawls below,
A sanctuary of green amidst the urban flow,
A walk to the top, a journey to the sky,
To witness London's beauty as the day goes by.

A sunrise climb, a gentle awakening,
The world below in hushed anticipation,
The city stirring, coming to life,
As morning light bathes in golden saturation.

And as the day unfolds, the sun climbs high,
Casting shadows, painting the canvas of the sky,
A symphony of colors, dancing in the air,
A masterpiece of nature beyond compare.

And when the day's work is done, and evening nears,
A sunset spectacle, with no need for cheers,
The city lights twinkle, a twinkling embrace,
A moment of peace in this bustling place.

Primrose Hill, a haven, a gem so rare,
A spot to pause, to breathe in the city's air,
To witness the beauty, the pulse of London
From the heights of Primrose Hill, our hearts are undone.

THERE IT SITS

There it sits off the shore
in the English Channel in Brighton.
The West Pier is a living,
breathing piece of art.

With the birds perching for a rest,
With sunrises and sunsets
basking in shades of colors
all around the black and ash
structure in the water.

The eerie fog rolls in
to surround the pier's structure,
making it feel even more mysterious.
But it is still a living, breathing piece of art.

In the quiet embrace of the sea,
it stands tall and proud,
a sentinel of times gone by
and dreams yet to unfold.

The whispers of history
echo through its weathered beams,
each crack and crevice
telling a story of resilience.

MEME LUKWITZ-MIHALOVIC

As the waves gently kiss its feet,
the West Pier remains steadfast,
a beacon of beauty and strength
in a world ever-changing.

And though the mist may shroud its form,
and the winds may howl in the night,
the spirit of the pier endures,
forever a masterpiece in sight.

FATHERS AND DAUGHTERS

The bond is something special,
unbreakable, undeniable,
a connection that transcends time,
a love that knows no bounds.

They say you tend to butt heads
with the parent you are most like.
Well, my father is stubborn,
so am I, but in that stubbornness,
we find understanding,
we find resilience,
we find strength.

He likes the water,
the gentle ebb and flow,
the soothing rhythm of the waves,
and so do I,
for in the water,
we find peace,
we find solace,
we find ourselves.

MEME LUKWITZ-MIHALOVIC

We agree that our humor is
very much the same,
a shared laughter that echoes
through the halls of our hearts,
a shared joy that binds us
in moments of lightness,
in moments of connection,
in moments of love.

Father and daughter,
two souls intertwined,
two hearts beating as one,
in this dance of life,
in this journey of love,
in this bond that is truly special.

MOTHERS AND SONS

We hold their hand for such a short time
Guiding them through the twists and turns of life
Watching as they stumble and rise again
Learning to walk, to run, to soar

We witness their first hesitant steps
Into a world that seems both vast and small
Their tiny hands in ours, trusting and unsure
As they navigate the path ahead

We stand by as they ride their bike away
Pedaling off into the unknown
Our hearts a mix of pride and fear
Knowing they are growing, changing, becoming

At 16 they grasp their driver's license
And we worry in a new way
Every time they drive away
Our minds filled with what-ifs and maybes

Then they find the one who holds their heart
And we watch as they intertwine their lives
Saying "I do" with tears and laughter
Starting a new chapter, a new journey

Mothers and sons, bound by love
A connection that time cannot sever
From first steps to new beginnings
We hold them close, always and forever.

MEME LUKWITZ-MIHALOVIC

GIRL DAD

Her first love is her dad,
He teaches her to respect herself,
He knows no one will love his girl more than her daddy.
Little girls soften their daddy's heart,
She will wrap daddy around her little finger.

In her eyes, he is a hero,
A protector, a guide, a pillar of strength.
He sees her as his princess,
A precious gem, a gift from above.

Their bond is unbreakable,
A love that transcends time and space.
He is her rock, her safe haven,
A beacon of light in her darkest days.

Girl dad, a title of honor,
A privilege to be cherished and revered.
For in the heart of a father and his daughter
Lies a love that knows no bounds, no end.

FATHERS AND SONS

Fathers need to remember
that one day his son will be following
his example more than his advice.
Encourage your son to talk to you.
As a father you may be his teacher,
but always remember you're his dad first.

In the grand tapestry of life,
where time weaves its intricate threads,
the bond between father and son
stands as a pillar of strength,
rooted in love and nurtured by wisdom.

A father's guidance shapes a son's path,
like a steady hand guiding a ship through stormy seas.
Yet words alone are not enough,
for actions speak louder than any sermon preached.

So let your deeds be a beacon of light,
illuminating the way for your son to follow.
Teach him the value of honor and integrity,
instill in him the courage to stand tall in the face of adversity.

But remember, dear father,
that your son looks up to you,
not just as a teacher, but as a role model,
a shining example of what it means to be a man.

So lead with kindness and compassion,
let your love be a shield against the harsh winds of the world.
And when your son looks back on his journey,
may he see in you the strength and grace of a father's love.

MEME LUKWITZ-MIHALOVIC

LOSS OF A FATHER

Losing your father is
To lose the one whose guidance
And help you seek
Whose support is that large and steady tree.

A towering figure, a beacon of strength
His wisdom like roots, grounding you in life
His love like branches, sheltering you from strife
His presence a constant, a source of immense light.

But now he's gone, a void left behind
An emptiness where his laughter used to chime
Memories flood in, bittersweet and kind
His spirit lives on in your heart and mind.

The loss of a father, a profound ache
A piece of you missing, a part of you breaks
Yet his legacy lingers, his lessons take shape
In the way you live, in the choices you make.

So cherish his memory, hold it dear
For though he may be gone, his love is near
In the whispers of the wind, the stars that appear
Your father lives on, forever and clear.

A FATHER'S LOVE

A father's love offers protection
In the world of unknowns,
A steady anchor in the storm,
Guiding with unwavering strength.

His love for his daughter grows stronger,
A bond forged in moments shared,
In laughter, tears, and tender care,
A love that transcends time.

Their connection evolves,
Shifting with the tides of life,
As she grows and changes,
He adapts, always there.

A father knows his place will shift,
As she finds her own path,
He'll stand by, proud and strong,
Yet knowing he must let go.

For one day, she'll find another,
A man who captures her heart,
And though his role may change,
His love will remain steadfast.

In the dance of life,
A father's love endures,
A beacon in the darkness,
Guiding her along the way.

MEME LUKWITZ-MIHALOVIC

MY SON, MY BEAUTIFUL BOY

I held you close and rocked you to sleep,
In the quiet of the night, your tiny breaths a melody.
I held your hand for such a short period of time,
Feeling the weight of your trust, the purity of your soul.

Then you grew, my son, and did not need me as much,
Your independence blossoming like a flower in the sun.
Now you are grown and on your own,
Navigating the world with courage and grace.

Just remember, my beautiful boy,
You will always be my baby, my heart intertwined with yours.
I love you, a love that knows no bounds,
A love that will carry you through life's highs and lows.

So go forth, my son, spread your wings and soar,
But know that my arms will always be open, ready to catch you if you fall.
You are my pride, my joy, my everything,
My son, my beautiful boy, forever cherished and adored.

TO MY ONLY CHILD

To my only child,
With you we share life's adventures
from walking the dog and talking
to flying away on a great adventure.
It is just the two of us against the world
With you, life is always a new adventure
That I look forward to.

In our little bubble of love and laughter,
We navigate the twists and turns of life
Hand in hand, heart to heart, soul to soul
Bound by a bond that transcends all else.

Together, we brave the unknown
With courage in our hearts and dreams in our eyes
Exploring the vast expanse of possibilities
In this grand tapestry of existence.

You are my compass, my guiding light
Leading me through the darkest nights
With you by my side, I fear no obstacle
For our love knows no bounds, no limits.

So here's to us, my precious child
In this wondrous journey we call life
May our adventures never cease
As we dance through the world, just you and me.

MEME LUKWITZ-MIHALOVIC

TO MY OLDEST

My first born,
You are the one who made me a parent,
The guinea pig, so they say,
Yet, you are the one whose smile enraptured my heart.

Your first kick made it all so real for me,
A parent, not something I ever thought I would be.
My first born,
My life began with you.

YOU SHINE

In the grand tapestry of life, you shine,
My oldest, my first born, my precious son,
You made me a parent, love so divine,
In your eyes, my journey had begun.

The guinea pig, they say, in this role,
Yet your smile captured my heart, pure and true,
Your first kick, a sensation to extol,
Brought to life dreams I never knew.

A parent, a title I never sought,
But with you, my purpose became clear,
In your gaze, a love that can't be bought,
My first born, my life began, my dear.

To you, my son, my guiding light,
In your presence, my world feels so right.

MEME LUKWITZ-MIHALOVIC

TO MY FIRSTBORN

My firstborn, my precious gift,
A guinea pig, they say,
But to me, you're the one who shifted
My life's compass, night and day.

Your smile, a beacon, bright and pure,
Enraptured my heart, so true.
You taught me what love could endure,
A bond unbreakable, just for you.

The laughter and the gentle touch,
The way you looked into my eyes,
You shaped me into the soul I clutch,
A testament to your love's prize.

Through sleepless nights and toddler years,
You filled my life with joy and light.
Your every milestone brought me tears
Of pride and love, a starry flight.

Now, as you stand, a youth grown bold,
I watch in awe, the man you've grown.
The guinea pig has played his role,
A journey started, a future known.

Your spirit shines, a brilliant flame,
A testament to all you'll be.
My oldest, my son, I'll always claim,
You're my first love, eternally.

TO MY YOUNGEST

My baby,
The one who completed the family.
You are the free spirit,
We just let you fly.
You never let us have a boring life,
No matter how old you may be.
My baby, you will always be.

Your laughter fills the air,
Your curiosity knows no bounds.
In your eyes, we see wonder,
In your heart, we find joy.

You dance through life with grace,
Embracing each moment with zeal.
A beacon of light in our world,
Guiding us through the darkest of nights.

You are the wildflower,
Unrestrained and untamed.
A reminder of the beauty of innocence,
A testament to the power of love.

My baby, my heart,
You are a treasure beyond compare.
Forever young, forever free,
Forever my baby, you will be.

MY DEAREST YOUNG ONE

In the realm of love, my dearest young one,
My baby, my joy, my heart's pure delight,
You arrived, our family now whole, spun
With laughter and mischief, shining so bright.

A free spirit, soaring high in the sky,
We watch in awe as you spread your wings wide,
Bringing color to our world, oh so spry,
In your presence, all dullness must hide.

No matter the years that pass us by,
In my eyes, you'll forever remain small,
My baby, my dear, my sweet little guy,
In my heart, you'll forever stand tall.

To my youngest, my baby, full of glee,
You've completed our family, eternally.

MY BEAUTIFUL GIRL

My beautiful girl
My baby girl
Not of my womb
But of my heart
You have and always will be
the daughter of my heart

In the vast expanse of love's embrace
You shimmer like a star in the night sky
Radiant and pure, a beacon of light
Guiding me through life's twists and turns

Your laughter, a melody that soothes my soul
Your eyes, like windows to a world of wonder
In your presence, I find peace and joy
A bond unbreakable, forged in the depths of my being

You are the essence of beauty and grace
A gift from above, a treasure untold
My baby girl, my heart's own delight
Forever and always, my guiding light

In your smile, I find solace
In your touch, I feel whole
You are the daughter of my heart
My love for you, an eternal art.

A MOTHER'S EMBRACE

From within your heartbeat's gentle beat,
A symphony that's forever sweet,
Your voice, a melody that fills my fears.

Your love, a force that gave me life,
A nurturing flame that eases my strife,
It guides my steps, a constant guide,
As I navigate this worldwide.

Your hand, a beacon in the darkest night,
A gentle touch that fills me with delight.
With every step, your love besides,
A steady presence, my unwavering guide.

Through life's adventure, come what may,
Your love will always light my way.
A guiding star, a constant gleam,
A beacon that fulfills my every dream.

YOU, MY MOMMA

In the quiet chamber of your womb, I listened
To the gentle thud of your heartbeat,
A rhythmic lullaby that whispered comfort and love.

Your voice, a melody of warmth and familiarity,
Echoed in the chambers of my soul.
The first song that I ever knew.

Your love, an invisible hand that cradled me,
Nurtured me, encouraged me to thrive
In the darkness of the unknown.

Guiding me through the maze of life,
Your love illuminated the path ahead,
A beacon of hope and strength.

Hand in hand, we navigate this world together,
Your love a steady anchor in the stormy sea,
A bond unbreakable, unyielding.

For in your love, I find my true north,
A guiding light that never wanes,
A compass that points me always back to you.

MEME LUKWITZ-MIHALOVIC

WHISPERING LOVE

In the vast expanse of darkness,
Inside the sanctuary of your womb,
I heard the symphony of your heartbeat,
A lullaby that soothed my soul.

Mommy, your voice was my first melody,
Whispering love and warmth,
Encouraging me to grow,
Nurturing me with every word spoken.

Your love, a force so powerful,
It gave me the strength to flourish,
To blossom into the world,
To take my first trembling step.

And as I navigate this vast unknown,
Your love remains my steadfast beacon,
Guiding me through life's twists and turns,
Holding my hand with unwavering grace.

Mommy, your love is my north star,
My guiding light in the dark,
A love that knows no bounds,
An eternal flame that burn brightly within me.

A SPECIAL CHILD

In the quiet moments of dawn's embrace,
I hold the gift of a special child close,
A grandchild who calls me Grandma with a smile,
A child so special, my heart overflows.

Their laughter dances like sunlight on water,
Their eyes filled with wonder and endless dreams,
In their innocence, I see a world untamed,
A world that sparkles with limitless streams.

I watch them play and hear their sweet voice,
A melody that soothes my weary soul,
Their tiny hands reaching for mine,
A bond that makes me feel whole.

I cannot wait to see them grow,
To witness the magic of their journey unfold,
For in their presence, I find pure joy,
A love that never grows old.

MEME LUKWITZ-MIHALOVIC

9 781665 761208